A Note to Parents

DK READERS is a compelling new program for beginning readers, designed in conjunction with leading literacy experts, including Dr. Linda Gambrell, Director of the School of Education at Clemson University. Dr. Gambrell has served on the Board of Directors of the International Reading Association and as President of the National Reading Conference.

Beautiful illustrations and superb full-color photographs combine with engaging, easy-to-read stories to offer a fresh approach to each subject in the series. Each DK READER is guaranteed to capture a child's interest while developing his or her reading skills, general knowledge, and love of reading.

The five levels of DK READERS are aimed at different reading abilities, enabling you to choose the books that are exactly right for your child:

Pre-level 1: Learning to read
Level 1: Beginning to read
Level 2: Beginning to read alone
Level 3: Reading alone
Level 4: Proficient readers

The "normal" age at which a child begins to read can be anywhere from three to eight years old, so these levels are intended only as a general guideline.

No matter which level you select, you can be sure that you are helping your child learn to read, then read to learn!

JP Wallace
Wallace, Karen.
A day at Seagull beach

JUN 0 7 '11

LONDON, NEW YORK, MUNICH,
MELBOURNE, AND DELHI

Created by Leapfrog Press Ltd.
Project Editor Naia Bray-Moffatt
Art Editor Jane Horne

For DK Publishing
Senior Editor Linda Esposito
Senior Art Editor Diane Thistlethwaite
U.S. Editor Regina Kahney
Production Josie Alabaster
Picture Researcher Liz Moore

Reading Consultant
Linda B. Gambrell, Ph.D.

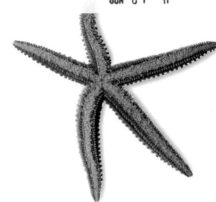

First American Edition, 1999
04 05 10 9 8 7 6 5 4 3 2
Published in the United States by DK Publishing, Inc.
375 Hudson Street, New York, New York 10014

Published in Great Britain by Dorling Kindersley Limited

Library of Congress Cataloging-in-Publication Data
Wallace, Karen
    Seagull beach / by Karen Wallace. -- 1st American ed.
    p.   cm. -- (Dorling Kindersley readers. Level 1)
    Summary: A seagull flies over the sea looking for something before
returning to its nest.
    ISBN 0-7894-4003-2 (hc). -- ISBN 0-7894-4002-4 (pbk)
    1. Gulls--Juvenile fiction.   [1. Gulls--Fiction..]   I. Title.
II. Series.
PZ10.3.W1625Se 1999
[E]--dc21   98-32291
                                                                    CIP
                                                                    AC

Color reproduction by Colourscan, Singapore
Printed and bound in China by L Rex Printing Co., Ltd.

The publisher would like to thank the following:
Key: t=top, a=above, b=below, l=left, r=right, c=center
Bruce Coleman: Gordon Langsbury front cover c; **Dorling Kindersley**
Picture Library: 1bl, 8-9tl, 20bl, 24tra, 24trb /Andy Crawford: 2br, 25 /Frank
Greenaway: 1tl, 4cl, 9b, 18tr, 18-19b, 28tl, 29br /Dave King: 1cla, 1br, 2tr, cr,
10-11, 13tr, b, 18tl, 21br, 24c, 28cr/Dave King/Natural History Museum: 14bl,
14-15b, 16-17b, 16tr /Susanna Price: 15tr /Matthew Ward: 1cra, 22tr, trb;
NHPA: 22-23b, 26br; **NHPA/Bill Coster:** 27; **Planet Earth Pictures:** Mark
Mattock front cover tr, cl; **Telegraph Colour Library:** 3br, 4-5b, 6tr,
6-7b, 9tr, 12tr, 15tl, 17tr, 19tr, 21bl, 26, 31tr; **Tony Stone Images:** front cover
background, 1tr, 5tr, 20-21tr, 20tl; **Tony Stone/Frank Orel:** 30-31b;
Tony Stone Images/John Warden: 1crb, 24br, bl
All other images © Dorling Kindersley.
For further information see www.dkimages.com

Discover more at

www.dk.com

DK READERS

BEGINNING TO READ **1**

A Day at
Seagull Beach

Written by Karen Wallace

DK

DK Publishing, Inc.

On a cliff above the seashore,
two sharp-eyed seagulls
build a nest.
They gather sticks
and bits of seaweed.

seaweed

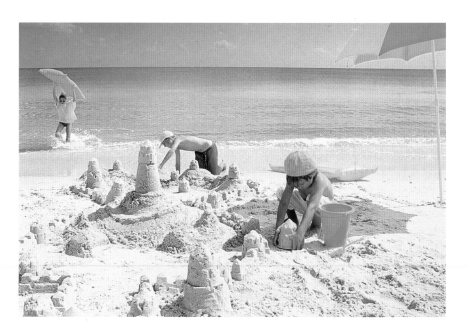

They watch the children
on the sand.

One seagull soars above the ocean.
The waves crash
on the seashore.
Whoosh! Boom!

The seagull skims the salty water.
What is the seagull looking for?

Seaweed flutters underwater.
Some looks like leaves.
Some looks like ribbons.

The sharp-eyed seagull
dips and searches.
What is the seagull looking for?

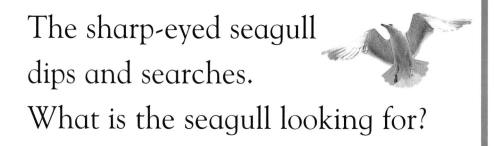

Down on the seabed,
a flat fish swims.

WIGGLE! WIGGLE!
He hides among
the pebbles.

TAP!

TAP!

The seagull walks
along the shore line.
TAP! TAP!
He pecks a crab's
hard shell.

SNAP! SNIP!
The crab waves
his sharp pincers.

pincer

What is the seagull looking for?

SNAP!

SNIP!

He hops behind
a slimy boulder.
He sees a rock pool
shining in the sun.

Inside the pool
a starfish creeps.

starfish

Nearby,

children laugh and play.

The sharp-eyed seagull
stands and watches.
A limpet clings to a salty stone.

limpet

What is the seagull
looking for?

A crab hides
in the seaweed.
The seagull waits...

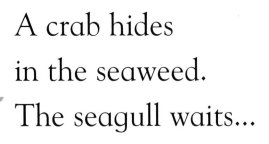

A pop-eyed prawn darts
through the water.

The seagull strikes!

His beak pushes
through the water.
Too late!
The pop-eyed
prawn escapes!

waves

The tide goes out,
the waves fall back.
A sandcastle sits
on the shore.

The seagull hunts among the seaweed. What is the seagull looking for?

He pokes and pecks
the shiny seashells.
They crunch and
tumble in the waves.

seashells

Some are straight, some are curly.
The seagull flips them
with his feet.

What is the seagull looking for?

He finds bits of glass
and polished stones.

He finds a hermit crab
and a jellyfish.

jellyfish

He sees a footprint in the sand.

What is the seagull looking for?

A fish tail flicks along a wave top.
Other seagulls swoop and cry.
SKREEK! SKREEK!

SKREEK!

SKREEK!

The seagull shrieks and snatches.
SNAP!
His beak is full of fish!

He's found
what he's been looking for!

eggs

On the cliff above the sea
the sharp-eyed seagull
lands by his mate.

She climbs off the nest.
He climbs on.
Two eggs
are lying underneath!

A seagull soars above the water.
She knows her eggs are
safe and warm.
She sees the children on the sand.

She skims along
the salty water.

What is the seagull looking for?

Picture Word List

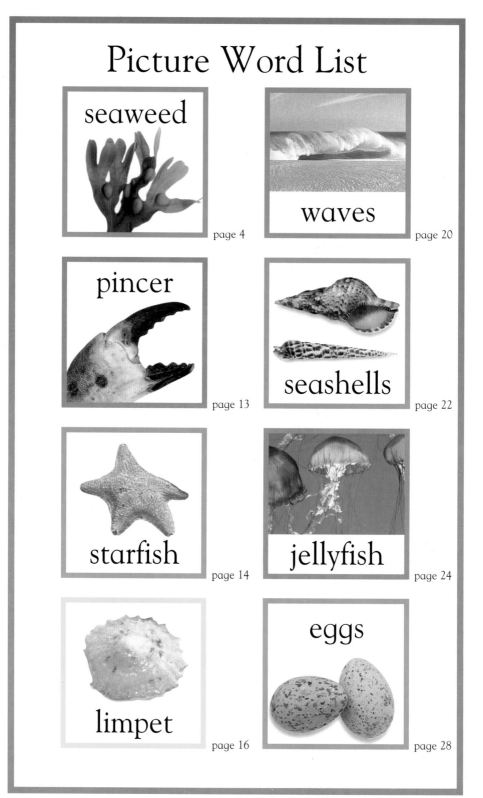

seaweed
page 4

waves
page 20

pincer
page 13

seashells
page 22

starfish
page 14

jellyfish
page 24

limpet
page 16

eggs
page 28